# coming to nothing

# coming to nothing

## Morgan Yasbincek

PUNCHER & WATTMANN

First published in 2023
Published by Puncher and Wattmann
PO Box 279
Waratah NSW 2298

https://www.puncherandwattmann.com
web@puncherandwattmann.com

ISBN    9781922571885

Cover image *ravaged dune 1* by Marion May Campbell
Cover design by Shaun Salmon
Typesetting by Morgan Arnett
Printed by Lightning Source International

A catalogue record for this work is available from the National Library of Australia

# Contents

## prose poems

# Psalm 21

*So teach us to number our days that we may apply our hearts unto wisdom*

here within an uncomplicated shape
wound into sightless black, like an adult mind in a
womb and going deeper, unborn squirming away from
groping ultrasound, this aversion
to announcements, declarations, pulls you under a surface
of yourself, identity a paper wasp
cell, spit and cellulose

cosmoses between atoms within molecules, platelets
tour the planetary, haemoglobin snatches life
from the sun, so forgetting is not a
loss but a return, burrowing impetus
weighty, gravity away from light, maximum
density of the empty dark a back-flip into
body disappeared

# sister

you stand in the well of night, sense the presence
of a boobook, a bowl of cold ash sits at your core, your palms
open their webbed lines, turn upwards, your face
turns too, supplicant

you've nursed family today, risen first and with those lined hands shaped
another day, kneaded them into tasks you will be paid for, driving, tapping
screens and tonight you stand listening for the presence, longing to see how
all of this has been spun, and from what

stars are a comfort – yes, they say, we see you by our
many-years-old light, with the light across years of moving night we see
you standing as one only, we see the bowl of ash, the upturned lines across
your hands, the sorrow smoothed into your still face

family calls, searching for you, and for a bracket of time you wait – she's
not here, they say maybe a walk – bowl of ash shifts, marri nuts, twigs crack
like low fire as you move over them, you walk down the driveway, boots on
gravel, past the weighty breaths of horses

halt at gate, inhale the wind from the south, from the mouth of night
look again before you breathe out – for you cannot be alone, and of
course, you are – to your left, to your right, at the cross-over
on each side stands a woman

# four poets and a horse reverse in Sapphic verse

chestnut nudges close as we stroke her muzzle
wants to follow, halted at gate-rail, standing
cocoa-powdered after her rolling, watches
after us, waiting

silken from her hosing, she'd found the pond of
dust, her forelegs ribboning, melting down to
capsize, kicking, groaning her pleasure skyward
freed from her halter

water sparking, shuddering droplets, belly
quivers, sprinkler-animal showers reaching
fingers, faces grimacing, wet relief in
afternoon's furnace

jarrah body, darkening honey, forelock
fallen shin-height, surrendered, licking open
handfuls, drinking overflow, eager poets
holding her jawline

Nandi begins hosing her fetlock, muddy
splashes, spotty, Marcella smoothing water
palms in motion circular massage, rinsing
coppery muscle

stance, relaxed in shadowy centre, calming
after stepping nervously uphill over
rusty furrows, following sandaled woman
nosing her shoulder

Scarlet anxious, Nandi's awakened dread of
hooves on toes in Birkenstocks marches out of
dragging pace, resisting then breaking
metronome dawdle

dozy after different poets' combing
brushing, mare in afternoon slumber, sighing
deep, announces a rhythm we've slipped beneath as
brushes delight her

redwood satin, hands on her, soothing gritty
sun-dried skin, Marcella has walked her up to
stable, Scarlet wondering, quiet, stranger's
confident movements

tied to railing, watery mane as blonde as
summer grasses, teenager knotty, stringlets
minutes ago, offering carrots, poets
meeting with mare in

jarrah dapple, palming the woody orange
roots in hands that separate language
into pieces, syllables into pixels
stitching their glimmer

# Carson Street

this time is our old testament, my daughter
strides the gravel circular drive, staff raised
above her head, shouting Pharaoh! – let my people go!

she cuts a length of string, measures me in cubits – four
and a bit, this solid brown cube of a cottage is our ark, sailing
the same seas as Jonah's whale

our house on the market, we save money on firewood by carving up
massive grey tree carcasses left on the vacant lot next door, wave
away the neighbour who patiently offers again to
start the miniscule chainsaw

we move into two new seasons without offers, prayer flags
faded to aqua and cream wave faint devotions into the sky
we live on vegetable soups, pastas, some meals
the child takes alone

our little round table a place to consider that first light, coming forth
like milk, we search every night sky for markings of these events
the wet print of cosmic waves that floated a planet to life's shore

we walk the dogs in the oven of afternoon, before the moon exists, pass
the house of the three Rottweilers, pocket carrots for Sarah, a lone bay
mare who leaves her evening mash of chaff and lucerne to come to the
    fence

this eight-year-old sings as we walk, she sings Adele, Lilly Allen
sometimes, sharing the way home, as sky bleeds the horizon, tiny
bats appear, tantalising our temples, ears, with almost-touch
like shadowy fey

the snake finally appears – a dugite driven towards the house by thirst, lifts
her head, assesses, beggar, blinded by torch light, she turns back
into the dark – sorry for her need, we place a bowl of water near the mound
of coffee rock she's become

# Burmese senryu

kitten gazes from
kelpie's bed, while dog struggles
foetal, on the cat's

*please don't kiss the cat*
*I'm just blowing in her face*
later, she shows me

work pants in wardrobe
cha-cha, buttocks swish, Zumba
cat drops through one leg

knocked off the bath ledge
dark-brown cat paddles
inevitable

on hind legs, tip toe
on towel rail, front paws reach, she
swings, try-out gymnast

she looks up, paws held
from daughter's lap, belly pelt
exposed, toes fanning

daughter's confidante
only she may enter there
without having knocked

morning rush, dogs in
*where's cat, she was here just now*
face in the linen

*what did you call out?*
*the dog's just eaten cat poo*
*oh no, I've kissed her!*

brown velvet curled on
plush teal, in half-dream, pink
leaf of tongue, dark purr

from the bush I bring
a feather, she carries it
off, newly moustached

# white grave

her last day, gripped tight by an exact measure of hours
resists the notches in the clock, push of leaking
seconds, against the wish it could melt, gush towards night

I guide her around the Buddha in the garden, kelpie
ears, two sleeves, open towards me, intent on following
collapsing hips fold in the heat, she climbs up off gravel

as we walk, I carry her grave within me, dug last night, down on river
flats beside our old weatherboard, a white hole in coastal sand, she'd
greeted me on return as if she could live fourteen more years
now I was home

this morning as I lined the boot of my car with a blue tarp, she lay in the
sun, one eye sliding, tracking actions, this strange mood, she'd sat
solemnly over suitcases, packing boxes, this day there's no anxious
shadowing, stealing into the car, sun has her buttered to earth

it takes some of the last of her life's effort to pull herself upward for the
circumambulations, black dog follows, an urgency, red knotted prayer
threads tied around her neck, the white grave, my voice an undulation
of mantras, we move through the hot air, she staggering to
follow my staggering lead

# magnificat

sitting across an equinox of sorts
in her bowl: dates, rosemary, goat cheese
wattle, blue leschenaultia in bloom
her voice is not high or questioning, nor
can she imagine herself as woman, she
holds that trapeze, wrist steady

she at her utmost, flush with breath
of another, full as a persimmon, accustomed to
visitation, yet alone in one choice and ready
to pivot a universe

# flame over chalice

inky wine sucks down the body of the flame, mirror's blade
of light, incandescent germ

wine alight with seed, pinned into life via stars and into them from
nothing, into that from the begetter of nothing
unalloyed gold cups liquid dark, yields this reflection
of which there is no other version

*ii*

darkness pours in, alive, slips the knot before time, bonds
with blood, takes her into the body beyond that veil, she recalls
the childhood devotions, visits to the playground grotto, sitting under
an unreadable Mary

each time she brought
a hurt life, if small, each time the message *I am here, continue . . .*

streams under the tongue begin to flow, saliva pours over the bed of the
mouth, urge to articulate arises, realises
all things wind into their resolution, loss also wreathes into
becoming, somewhere lightless, familiar, the pouring and drinking
life for its own sake, love for its own, how a passing of a sun changes
every living and inert thing

*iii*

wine vapour pinkens aura of flame, rose-gold spheres
over the chalice, dawn's reach just before sun crowns
to be held in the column, vent of breath, is to be marked
– only death is no one

*...reproach.*
*...delicate*
*...Artemis*


Sappho, streams flow from my arms to yours, are of
the warmer colours, you are still
the only one who can get past my dogs

you come to me with poet's questions, they
fly into me faster than my own arrows – do
not bring your lyre, or wine, no matter how spiced

I am at risk of begging to swap places, unhook the great crescent
from its mooring, drop my bow into its hull and float
downstream, covered in mortal skin

I long to see your room, lift its delicate jars and fabrics over
fingertips, drink mint liqueur, sleep with
your palm across my heart

*Dead you will lie and never memory of you*
*will there be nor desire into the aftertime – for you do not*
*share in the roses*
*of Pieria*


fifty daughters, abandoned by
good Greek sons carrying woad felt shawls, flowers, baskets, who
unrolled meagre packs

to show they left with nothing, oh wasted years, they
cried, oh the frustration of having to nurse roses in
this drought-ridden place

their children face their last sight of the men, a woman
holds their heads to her now, sorrow streams across her palms, thorns
point at her, she digs, loosens roots to uptake more water, composts

kitchen waste to feed them, coaxes them to feed, pinken
when they close into sleep she sits at her table, listens
to the clock, waits for the mares

they arrive; she catches one at a time with the cord
from her waist, locks them in her yard, they nose
wild oats, clover, lavender – tell her about her children, the hard buds
of their grief, as she pulls burrs from their manes

settles them under skin of her hands, hours later full-bellied mares stream
from the yard, gallop towards brightening edge of night, leap
another horizon

*do not move stones*


because they must outlast
the circumstances of their
placement, cannot articulate
the value of their charge, arrange
the vowels of silence, because landscapes
could not have imagined
them, they're best left
best left

*They say Leda once found a hyacinth-coloured egg hidden*

did the woman who found the egg
settle it on heartskin, protect the shell from
cooling, find she loved its secret forming, bind it, sleep
with pillows tucked so even unknowing could not harm

did it float the dark, between her breasts, sail her breath, rhythms
below shape a downy embrace, in which tenderness grew its
helix, and when the creature quivered, did it ripple through to
the very tips of the woman

when the chick tapped out, black-purple and wet-warm
olive beak at rest on woman's sternum, did her down, fine as
kitten fur, dry to an amethyst glow

when the lavender cygnet
made utterance, did she announce night would reside on the
other side of her feathers, that she would bring the woman
stars to eat, did she name the woman day, say

I am thought by some to be a white swan
flying into twilight, by others black swan flying
into dawn, but you know I am the colour of red turning
blue, blue turning red, blood and breath, and with that
did she open the grown span of wings over the
woman, leave her in the brilliance?

*...with what eyes*

what eyes look upon us first, what minds in the room, what
gossamer wafts its truth there, with what eyes do we
wake, what dreams silt them

with what eyes does the cat study you as you step
from the shower, from the chair next to you as you write

once in the lab we cut open the eyeball
of a bull, retina iridescent navy silk, life of seeing
lined with emptiness, every dissection slips out what
is sought, reveals

the nothing, did you never prise off your doll's head, nose into its
small bowl of earthen light, find her ...
gone

## ECHO – SAPPHO

*I would not think to touch the sky with two arms*


but to hold her to me, welcome
my elder sister, riding the crown
of the sun through fathoms of pink

magpies pipe
their full-throated effort as she arrives, stepping
through icy stars
dripping light

*do I still yearn for my virginity?*

she arrives unannounced after each birth, shares the first night's
vigil, lays her veil over me, we watch our baby dreaming
on the other side of her eyelids

her tiny face converses in sleep with a place
before, kisses, suckles in dream, her father
sleeps, doesn't welcome our guest

she visits between lovers, contrives for us to go
out, takes me to the sea at night, we swim wickedly in
black water outside the circle of light from a boutique hotel

it's a joke between us of course, the idea
one of us could be taken; stolen or lost, unthinkable
that I could *give* her to anybody

after a pregnancy dissolves into air she walks
with me, says, for now
the whole of this life
is an empty room

*someone will remember us*
*I say*
*even in another time*


today I leave the touch of my daughter's
sleeping hand, smoothed
in the dark this morning by my own

stroked her jaw with my other hand and whispered
low, so she wouldn't wake but would stop
grinding her teeth

her face did not still, hand twitched in mine
held her to me under the blankets, trying to find
the code to cast peace through her sleep, protect her
from what must come upon her

*But I am hardly some backbiter bent on vengeance; no, my heart is lenient*

lenient heart has that wide, heavy-hinged back door, caretaker
sweeps untreated boards, damp dusts crevices – moths, lizard skins swept
out, she props it open with the broom – for a high wind to blow
through

it hears the creatures of the deep move and cry in tidal silences
of conversation, after exhalation, magnifies tensions, strains of
intonation, detects abandoned nests, takes rest at night in the still's
overlay of renewal, listens to the mopokes leave their posts on the
driveway, hears the stars set

their nets, is willing to
consider a world
without it, cultures
emptiness from harvested breath

---

Title quotations taken from *If Not, Winter: fragments of Sappho*. Anne Carson, Vintage Books, New York, 2003.

# three poems for Fay Zwicky

*black swan of tuonela*

clan of stately magpies skip, like sisters, over your
wall, tap your window, we will not leave they say until
you sing back, breathe more words under our sky

not for you the croaking emissaries of a dark male
god, they've come to sing you through the pillars of
black and white, get up and walk, they chime, yours
is a distant celestial track

we're hiding in the reeds, not ready, you say, as we go
under again, walk the river bottom, labour through mulch
of sand, algae, dumped building rubble, frilly brown
jellyfish pump speckled petticoats

crabs wave and run, your oxygen tube gurgles
along behind, you step around it, break out of the
cordoned off space of dying woman, pull up stone after
stone, body parts of memory, your fingers sift and rake
the dark

at last you swim out, released from reeds and mud, your
exhalation, scores smooth folds over water, white under-
feathers form a cloud-cushion for your reflected double

she swims the sky, no line of cygnets in tow, hooks at the tips of
her scarlet feet drag twilight over water, she folds her head deep
into pocket between rib and wing, drifts from a shore she has forever left

*visitors*

cat sits at my knees while rain colours in windows, wind
bangs heads of trees together, at the bottom of the hill
I buy lavender chrysanthemums, apricot lilies from a man who
runs a smile to my window under an open umbrella in heaving rain

leave them with your son at the ward desk, he cradles them
along his forearm, like a newborn, his kind words
reveal I have seen you
for the last time

on way back across the city then out the
other side, glad of the veils of water, car a red fish
riding a current, hoping you knew
that Blake died singing

at home, a candle lit, watch the cat sit after eating, her tiny pink
tongue, fine as a pinch of ham, swiping and sweeping over her
cheeks, left paw lifting, she circles it over her plush dark brown
face, then sits, blinking

*in the end*

we kneel, pour out all we have collected, we all
have to empty our pockets

then we stand to look around, joining the horizon
into a circle

will you dance then in that place
holding the instrument you have learnt to play?

will you call your dog to follow – or wait for the
company of stars?

you will be utterly alone, the only human, before the quiet draws
you forward once more, so that in the beginning you will

collect your balance from the waters, rise up to standing, walk
looking for the sun, while your world dances around you

# Rose of Wilyabrup after the spring concert

her glass sits under her face, its bowl catches her words – she
is saying she doesn't know what it was that knocked her off
her pedestal but her flamenco is brilliant – and you can see her winding
under the call of her castanets, as she stamps all the way into
her hips, turning below snaking hands on drumming feet

rains have come late, bumped into the next
season, so now seems the time to taste the spring in a
wine the colour of a late summer twilight

in the storm light she is somehow lit by this tincture, its colour
nothing like the mixing of red and white, a cordial but not
a plasma, an ethereal pink floating over the sea
at the close of a forty-three-degree day

my youngest, grown too soon into a swan
floats on pointe, her feet silk-ribboned into this same colour
as her arms lift the tips of her fingers onto the shelf of flight, she spins
through girlhood with six others and with necks craning, faces to the sky
they beat their wings against it and beatific, hatch themselves one by
    one

my friend has swapped ballet for flamenco, keeps
wishbones on her windowsill, each bone holds a wish in its Y
to be snapped free, as long as two are willing to take the risk of letting it
    fly
to the other

# pre-dawn in march

3.50 am or so, that magnetic light's called
through the window, sliding the brain open

paddocks are rectangles of clay dust
wind, a liberated intention, washes me
in air

in pyjamas under a punctured moon, thin layer of stars, I open
the gate, horses examine me with their
nostrils, crunch lucerne twigs out of my hands, canter into the hay

scarred face whispers through the grill of her stereotype
of searches for a lost sister, haunts
a love none below understand

she tattoos shifting pictures over herself, manages to
convey her loss to someone awake at this hour

but my boots are not made of the sun, they're simple black
rubber, the horses spend their love on hay

my hands are empty, the stars are sparse, we all hear her cry into the wind

# Sevillana

*For Esther*

four years so far – re-enacting the net
of steps, rhythm sonars down through legs, each six
beat cycle announced by a collective stamp, 'break' sends
low boom along floorboards, muscle memory reaches for
trace, lost between knowing and unknowing

Andalusian mare swings my hips into her
big gait, trots through our castanet cycles, arms
lower and rise in the exact arc of the music box
ballerina, horse avoids gravel margins, prefers to strike
surer surface under hoof, tightens her gait, it
claps against the eucalypts

this dance began when my daughter was still
lost, teacher's hands on shoulders that would not be pulled
out to lift chest, imply pride, imitate passion, shoes
bit deep into untempered feet

last saw you in the land where whole villages rise
into this dance, we stood in the turret of the unfinished
cathedral, our families still forming, our noses reddening
in the cold heights of it, before that we danced to *I will survive*
in Edinburgh basement nightclub, aglow in red wine gothic, blue
lit version of you banished phantoms, left hand on hip, right finger
pointing them out the door

you sleep as I write, the pod of your home
drifts through lockdown, stymied by howling coastal
sleet, tomorrow for you is 'a jab and chips', words
ignite with the glow of common prayer, in this
hemisphere I stand in the last third of a hay roll
heart to heart with my
deep-chested mare, a jab and chips

eventually, others will dance on the
complimentary diagonal, when the elusive
duende is pleased enough, but for now
our globe with her great cheek resting on an axis
is about to roll over, enter another
dream

---

duende – an elf spirit drawn to guide in dance, pertaining to the Flamenco

# The twelfth year

*God is the circle whose centre is everywhere and circumference is*
*nowhere* ~ St. Bonaventure

this land, Nyoongar, *Whudjuk*, has lifted many lives to the sun
of all its trees, a silver Gungurru, remembers this:

fat wrens jive and hop, attracted to the children
their pear-wood flutes

tree stands luminous from rain, dangling light ribbons drape their play
as they learn of the house of their becoming:

it floats on a celestial sea, each of its bricks fired in human effort
pod of darkness, coordinated
to receive light, when it descends blood will rise
grow children

they look out from their constellations, wonder
at the hands of human life

in the marri stand many small hands frantic with promise
build house after house and a village of branches, twigs and coffee
rock forms, it runs on a currency of pinecones and from this grow
the wealthy, the gatherers and the homeless –

shops appear in the village selling necklaces of coloured
macaroni, found threaded treasures, exotic leaves, honkey
nuts and sticks, there are slaves and thieves
law givers, police and prisoners

some days the children are kept away from the village, its pull
tearing at the calm of their rhythms, its drama
knocking on classroom doors

then they might go down the hill, eat foamy cerise lilly pillies
or mash the whole school together in a game of British bulldog

they learn how shadows measure time, follow Moses through the desert
 – with their staffs raised above their heads they cry *let my people go*

an Irish boy, lean as a pedlar sings them forward, his high sweet voice
opens the sky, then they cross into the Ramayana, the abduction of
Sita, the demon who dies upon the lament of good he might have
done, expose their hearts like Hanuman, offer them to the sun and pray
for grace to touch their day

by day their teacher leads them into new dances, her voice the
channel of their seeing, by night she considers each child in the quiet
her pilgrims recite her verses for them
stepping into them until they walk into new colour

they are her array, she their centre, and they follow the rootlines
of the tree as they leave its shade for their grown lives, their hands
newly powdered in silver

# why do you wake me

why do you wake me, empress of sky, your hair
awash in nebulae as you stride the breadth of the exosphere
drag your glistening net over the horizon

I watch you cure your haul, drying racks of constellations
in accordance with human ripening, whisper soothing calculations
into the throats of volcanoes

why so enamoured of this earth, wet and messy in your lap
so patient with her pre-teen civilisations, waiting for time
to tutor their unruly compositions

you sleep with us women, your body the dark exhalation
giving succour to suns, and for the bereft insomniac you
leave as a lantern one star cooling in its cage and a silk weave
from the Bay of Dew

at your table a veracious fish spills rubies onto plates, murmurs
into the cups, prompting them to conceive colour, while the forgotten
gather; ancestors turned to shadow, the exiled
wise, the broken and amnesiac

you walk without cloak or broach or face, protectress
of the reverent, your feet washed in milk, your tropical temperament
calms the distressed, your vespertine secrets bless
the banished, lift us out of genuflection and usher
us back to the tasks of living

every queen has knelt before you on a stone floor
to receive cup, wand, sword and crown, every saint has sought
your counsel, given as the early light through the tallest chapel
window

# that day

next door flies the flag all year, down by their front gate, lips
of their starving horses stay down in the dust, mouthing rocks, dung, nicker
to us at the fence for smuggled hay and carrots
city mind erects thousands of flags, twin flags on cars, diplomats

of a pretend country, traffic patterns intensify, populations mobilise
move into position, set up deck chairs, fence themselves
in with eskies, pop-up tables

untethered dogs wander beach carparks
mosaics of coloured duco, music trapped in houses, cars
punches at windows, a hundred thousand arms spread blankets, elbows
wide, selfies bubble across the ether, wires plug into bodies, boom boxes

thunder words like 'proud' 'Australian' nobody dies in explosions
of light – massacres, tied to the stones of history, lie quiet
this is a day of celebration, intoxication, glassing assaults, rape

a day when some Australians stand together
to wave a plastic flag

# what food?

some kind of meat, someone who has
birthed young, lain hammocked in the
darkness between breaths, one body
pulled into two

punished by unknowing, illiterate, chewing
through light into dark, one who gives voice
inside mists, along with chuck-a-lucks and koolbardis

creature of this architectured green, of
other lands too – imported, branded; four limbs two eyes, two
ears, two nostrils

milk taken from beyond offspring, them taken too, their calls
caught in paddock stones, bumping against light, none allowed
to grow old, we walk the ramp into shadow

dissected in advance, hefted under armpits, wind
hooks me up, I hang from the fat wrinkly branch
of the lemon-scented gum – chest brisket, buttocks
top round, broken on a jarrah table
neat sign spears miniature real estate
100% organic – grass-finished

# wild caught

once, the cold eye
cast a peregrine
falcon
into the teeth
of my car at one
hundred k's, deep
teal flash, plunging
for a wagtail, little
bird dipped a moment
into metal torrent

buried
in bushland, it was
as a replica, sculpted
ether

# community

*for N*

forty degrees, forty of us in the unpowered Jewish temple, gateway
to the burial lawn, raw concrete gazebo, exposed unpainted wood
rudimentary skylight

bodies blacken to life-shapes against intense, invasive light
inside, a few concrete benches, tidy set of three short pews for inner
family, women's side of the rope barrier

men in kippas pack into their half, stance dutiful, women churn
theirs; stand up, sit down, find another face, continue sentences begun
months before –

so what did you end up doing with that piano … meant to let you know
Michael did his back in … oh there's Julie … others lean arms in
to the only ones seated, all make fans of their service sheets

Rabbi, beard to his sternum, too young to really
be the authority here, says he realised something about love when
he met the widow this morning, but elects not to share

brother of first wife tenderly summons the man whose last exhalation
was fifteen hours ago – mentor, father, a ballet dancer, an artist
new widow isn't friends with all this, seems irritated with its labour
bolts through the guard of honour as if she doesn't see it

after her we walk out across the single line of square headstones
laid flat in the lawn, path of ancestry of the common, we step
over the names, each held by a brass star of David

'please not on the grass'

his grave a yellow hole above another who looks through the eyes of
their three children, three grandchildren, bubbles into interior jostling
one makes a joke about who's on top

coffin's lowered by relatives, then after a hesitation due to respect and
the heat, a communal shovelling, our widow leaps off the path first
in a surge of energy, rapidly empties several loads of yellow sand, it
sounds against hollow pine like
someone gently knocking

# thirty-three hours

don't come in, don't want you to
catch . . . so we said our last words on your
driveway

barefoot on the freckled brick paving
pale blue pyjamas, complexion of aged cream, your talk
anxious – maybe bit of a bug, clear soup a boiled egg, still

some pain, left side, where you'd landed
worried, you said, after all the blueprinting for a retirement, now with six
days to go . . . tests were clear, we affirmed again, nothing

broken, doctor unconcerned

thirty-three hours later sitting with your body, an inert curl on the spare
bed, your green eyes cast down, mannequin stare, hair damp – vomit wiped
my legs jump to standing every few minutes

he's very ordinary, your favourite summing up, meaning
safe, but words on age difference had sent you
cycling into a rainy dusk, crossing the equinox

pedalling against your own
tide, 'til the maroon car dislodged the scales, jettisoned
you

tests were wrong tests, your pain read
upside-down, and between us zones of
reassurance, child / parent, where darker bloods don't

mix, standing apart . . . in case
until the 2.15 am phone and something the size of a small boulder falls
from the ceiling onto my chest, pushes me half-way through the
    mattress

## another dream

again and again waking is disembarking into
another dream
before natural light filters in, before the people of
the dream have received their 'wet box', deeply sown
with seeds, baby cos lettuce already sprouting, the mattress rolls
like a wave as you move to get up

*cantaloupe* is the word that haunts today, possibly exhaled by its
submerged seed, was the fruit hunted for at the grocer, but
it lurked like a concealed head and would not come to mind

# reflection

her mirrors stand empty
she takes direction from need for
water, showers the mint, tomatoes
repairs the horse trough

uninterrupted by any future
she walks across the dust
looks into the broken well, flash
of light on water

someone there
looks over the rim
hair drapes petals around her face
fingers curl on the lip, toes turned to clay dust
behind, a star – white-hot sun
looks for a way in

# little sea goat

she climbs, cloven grip on shore and stone, each
step ignites compulsion to climb, life below increasingly
sanctified by scale and silence
appetite thinned by altitude to a yen for alpine herbs
winkled out from between boulders
as she climbs the giant, the sky shortens its margins to
horizontal beam
she trots across her own equinox into adolescence
vanishes in the steamy clouds

# bad shoulder

governor of the pillar of severity, unserviced, unbalanced
machinery left dry in times; propped, fixed, tampered
wires tangled, too many loads

weighty children, heads nestling into the joint, tens
of thousands of kilometres bracing steering wheels, tugged by
dog leads, lifting dishes, pulling drawers, locking and unlocking
doors, sliding

the mouse, yanking trolleys, prams, hauling school bags, shopping
recycling, heaving garden rubbish, bags, buckets of earth, water
chaff, lighting candles, catching the cat, typing hundreds
of thousands of words, a fraction of them her own

she was the one who trained, copied the letters from the blackboard,
    pages
of small 'a's, 'm's, strange numerical 'z's, lower case, capitals, cursive,
    then
lines of them through assignments, poetry, letters
painting the house alone before

the wedding – broken family promises
buckets of dark rose, turmeric-gold limewash
going off, right arm spasming at 3am

what if it had been let go, maybe if there had been writing instead of
suffering, what if she had hurled the buckets of colour down the
hallway or lifted them high and poured them over the windscreen
of the cars of the promise-breakers, or

driven them into the Italian cafe where barista husband-to-be worked
and poured them into the fountain in the middle of the restaurant
what if she had refused to become the bad shoulder

she would not be encased, twisted, inflamed, now the weaker arm, 'bad'
arm, the other will never be able to butter bread properly, lay out
numbers on a page, she's written, held, convened, become the leader
the one who moves first

first to hold the pencils, held yellow up for the approval of the eyes – they
especially liked yellow – was the first to lay them carefully side by side in
the metal pencil box
close the lid

# uniform fitting

racks of navy and white clothing wait in plastic film
parents sit against a wall on one line of cream plastic chairs

four pop-up dressing rooms eject boys and girls, they walk away from
the cubicles briskly primary school years already crumpling into a
gestating past, an allotment, childhood

one girl is bent like a bow by her own height, long brown hair drags
her head forward, she stands beside her father, the shirt she's trying
falls past her wrists, she talks to him with her hand in her hair, another
who could pass for eight, works through the process independently
apparently without the presence of a parent at all.

boys are, anonymous, baggy, for them it's a swift process: they nod to
their mothers as they walk through the curtain, the mothers fold layers
of navy plastic over their arms, they walk out in unison

girls watch girls, nervous as prey

she's a size eight . . . no, aaate, she doesn't want that one, it's too big –
all attention's on a two-metre-tall twelve-year old girl who wears a
rainbow bandeau around her hips, a bikini top, thin-strapped thongs
she carries along a mother in runners and baggy t-shirt, an older sister
with hair of calendula gold

they argue on her behalf with the navy woman from the uniform
company while the girl manoeuvres her thumb over the screen of her
phone

oh but she's so tiny, that's way too big for her, it doesn't matter if she
grows out of it, we can always buy a new uniform – not of the ones who
dropped several degrees of humour when going over the price list

for those of us who had hosted a jolly chat with our daughters about the
culture of purchasing uniforms; everyone in first year has a somewhat
oversized start, of course it won't be a sack but no-one can afford to buy
every year . . . it's all over;

there will be tears in the pay queue, baggy t-shirt mum and calendula
sister will choose a layer of kind words about how good this school is
utterly free of how they have unpicked our options, stimulated the
secret violence pinching and grabbing at our shirts

galvanised declarations of refusal from the back seat
on the way home are directed at drivers who would place
their own in the crosshairs of imperfection

# who would dare

decapitate this Buddha, whose black
volcanic skin surprises touch
with living warmth

sat here eleven centuries, right palm perpetually
stretched open to us, fingers reach toward the earth in
wish granting mudra, siphon

infinity through the vast expanded heart
beating there, that smile
now everywhere

# be gentle breath

be gentle sky, don't let the
dust inside, no sorrow to be
had alone, no grief to find in bone, it's
all held in life, coming strangely like
the branches of night

quiet sense it's impossible to be alone, loves
pattern every silence, simple fact of a loved
one dead, emptiness
of a sky
that was last night a custard of cloud

# faith

surrounded by ravens, they call the word 'inevitable' over the
top of the house, sharp, brazen

like the worst landlords they have entered without knocking and
they will leave when they have eyed the block blade by blade

to the height of the treetops, surveyed our lives down
to another word, which they drag between them as they lift

for three weeks, just before summer storm the Carnaby's
make camp in the backyard, chewing marri nuts, shredding fluffy
lemon and cream flowers

kookaburras scream awake the heat, their lunatic wails from the
masts of dry trees bring the sun too fast into the sky

ring tones of the bronze-wing go unanswered day and night – the low
    notes
of an insomniac owl, we think, until we spot the buxom dove, tail
    extending
and releasing, her painted face expressionless

# Thomas

one who needed to touch, who entered
the wound, affirmed at fingertip
electric recognition

those who have hugged the dead in dreams, or
touched a wound on a loved body newly
changed, may not see him woven in simply as the
doubter, but as one who stepped forward when beckoned
to assure himself of living skin

# born of a number

the twenty-eight living at this café is overconfident
and tubby, will sit on your table and eat from your hand

sitting on the sofa outside the café, it's now closed
had to insist on getting in, doors locked
twenty minutes early, loud music, blinds pulled, patient
knocking, eventually purchase a long mac, piece of carrot cake
for a daughter on her way up the hill by bus

she remembered me into a future and I remembered her
into a past, we lived by the sea, sweltered in the haze of longer
days sipping lemon water, we both resumed life in images

today is the day of the tubby twenty-eight and scooting
bandicoot joeys whizzing around bushes, inky clouds
pile up in the sky like liquorice ice cream, older people
who come to the counter allow little facial
movement, person-shrinkage behind the skin, then
the quick twinkle response
to a smile, symphonic lustre

# what colour, treachery?

not black, that emptiness before
conception, afterward of empty
cave-dark room, peace in which
monks vibrate voice of a planet
tunnelling endless song of didgeridoo

nor purple, doesn't need to belong, strange
colour of heat at night, water stars arrive in
could be red, not jewelled birth-red, futility rage red
it's more cowardly than red
more human than colour

# Magdalene

single witness for
the sake of those who search and wait, silk-fine
cord upon which a world turns
the point time cannot move

winds fly from her hands across the desert, she
moves camp to camp, stands tall while
the homeless sleep, coiled and brittle as shellfish

she is the flame in the wine, light
in the blood, honey in the roots
embedded, alive

# grief's ice burn

glacial layers slide through soft core, distend
muscle, bruise cartilage, snap ligaments, a wake
cleaned of life, a gnawed bone

skeleton folds like plasticine, resident
forces cannot accumulate
to form resistance, will
has no penetration but sits like a light
snow, lifting off in hard wind like
feathers discarded
from fox kill

# woman on the train

a supermarket cooler bag
on her lap, a knife, an orange

she spoons the juice from the
orange into her mouth

she wears a lanyard that says 'do not disturb', holds
herself with elbows into sides, concentrated over
her nest of bags, slowly hatching
the aroma of orange

# child light

child-light descends today, as
her milk comes in, links the two with
fine streams of bluish-white water, movements are
developing a rhythm, one not yet graceful
around this fresh bright need

the quiet hours are now occupied, bumped
out of sleep, there are visitors, delighted
already, hurrying with warm loaves, cakes
under tea-towels

everything consumed is made of light, phases
of time blend, melt into a sea of its moving, set
afloat a family, somehow steady
in the eye of time

# spider

one of our last meals together
our torsos cut in half by the faux wood Laminex
table – not clean enough for you

waitress, moved by the sting of your criticism slaps
the table with a sour-smelling cloth, leaves circular swirls
of moisture under our plastic plates

a black spider dead on the floor beside my chair, legs curled, inside
the weaving begins: bloodless nights at the table with a pissed
scowling stepfather the silent push against words, searching for a vein
of life to float words on, the hope that conversation could
flower with the opportunity of a shared meal

we are all in the cavern of your aura, the waitress, the spider
and me – the dishes are homogenised by it, sliced celery, carrots
Chinese cabbage, some blonde sauce, steamed
rice, the plates seem to all be full of the same thing, one flavour

though I have known for years that I never wanted
to be here again, I find a tolerance, like a trained animal

# handless maiden

she eats pears as she moves through your poems
– one bitten by a cat, one bruised
from just sitting in the bowl – everything is gripped
by her jaws, palms resolved into a tongue

not everything has to be saved, you say

for some reason the branches don't agree
they make their fingers into fruit, star
flowers empty their centres, cores of
red, green, gold, colour vital organs
– liver-dark plums divide like hearts
flush like kidneys, thread like
veins

teeth slice through fibre, filaments weed
the mouth, it becomes a sea cave of
fruit tendrils

here, say the trees, have my hands as they
pick threads from her mouth with finger
twigs, eat them, so she continues, spitting
stones back into the ground
foresting her way

# talisman

I carried you
you were heavy within me calling
to the earth
I am always waiting for you to
appear, as if this time
we could complete

that old dog never returned
we waited, didn't let anyone else
drink from her bowl
she trots through me when the air becomes still

she tells me you are there, on that different
horizon, level with the sun
you walked into the end of life, a
woman rushing at her glass reflection
it absorbed you, leaving only an impression
of a red dirt sky

we all have a road in and a road out, so
the conversation went – yes, you said
walking only slightly lop-sided
you set traps for anything shadowy, scrubbed
clean your last page, leaving a single pointing
sign, its indications slightly frayed

avoided checking your fingernails, not
wanting to see your body grow without
you, yet now inwardly – most of them, their
unfeminine thickness, curve
clipped back just short of claw

ridge dividing the right thumb
a cut to the quick when your father
insisted it be you to hold the wood
on the block

somehow you made months
with cancer episodic, found a
thread in it, using optimism as
a spindle, even then it was slippery –
endings, beginnings lost in the twist
of it, grateful, you said, newly made, tour
guide for the options, but as you
prepared for yearly tests fear
dropped its net over your face, your hand
would reach to your throat and the faint
muscles under skin would flutter, fold wings
in tight.

you brought home the aqua mesh mask from radiation
therapy, sat it on the bookshelf behind your chair, where
level with your shoulder blades, it watched you

I dreamt there were two where there should have been one
you were calling, but your voice never made it across the break between
we had no way of finding one another, but for the sense, somewhere, of
having been promised light

one day this will be me, or at least
some atoms of me watching you try to work out who I am

standing, you became a living fossil
waiting for your bones to be brushed, tapped
hatched into your first interpretation

red-tailed black cockatoos claim the marri
nuts, hokey pokey in the eucalypt fronds
drop nuts onto the roof and single feather, molten
red brilliance, just one, always a talisman

grass, smoke, bloody skies and a season
without butter, its early cool chopped out
as though the night could only deliver a sun
mid-morning

you said your grandmother
could fly, that she still nests in her favourite tree

my hands are not big enough, but
my roots are big enough to hold you

we used to remember, but now we're making something
else into colour, (this woman knows what she can
do with time) the way
 – from
here              to here
you will always belong

before the river divided the tree made itself into a door

what is left of us is base layer, but for
ridges made by currents, like whorls of a
fingerprint
there is space for you here
no matter what is left

_____

A response to RAW exhibition, Perth Oct 2021

# Raven

first, a declaration
reply informs of its mistake
ohh, it says, aaahohhh
raising objection
flies off, crying
anyway, anyway

# lunar eclipse

we camp between the breast to breast
gargantuan embrace between earth shadow and
bleeding moon

frogs drop their yells to a murmur, stars hurriedly
funnel their lights downstream, something
mighty happening

a woman enters the water, on her way
to join the turtles, feet slide in silt
muck, gravel bones

is that someone paddling, I wouldn't
there'll be snakes

there's no snakes

still, it's the dark water

yes, she thinks, it's the dark water, no stranger

it severs her head before she goes under
beneath the dark amber lunar coal

she rises back into air through film
of waterskin to wait with snakes, paperbarks
mosquitoes
in the sky emerging, receding, crowning
dome of molten gold, seam of white as
they let go

two ducks water-ski, hiss twin
lines of silver over the lake

# fool

at the end of my feather, last one so
most precious, nothing's a perfect fit
anymore, somehow got here in wrong
shoes, old slippers really, few layers of
dresswear, not right for this steep
cold climb

one red feather, now in my
pocket, last of spring colour
focusing a point ahead
a pinnacle, highest
I dare to climb in damp slippers
leaking white padding

toes a fuzz of ache, layered leggings, pants
kimono jacket make a creature comforting
a secret, the jewelled last and it will raise the
most voice I have, against rushing wind, astonish
those kiting the thermals, will fancy a song
with instrumental voice, encourage the venture to
rapture, hell-bent on light

ever so deeply . . . more deeply the higher
this aching does sing, the knowing of how an entire
existence formulates a circumference around
simply letting the last feather go

with an exhalation

the span of looking across
the chasm a climb has made, the
holding inside
a radiance

# accident

not that you could make it happen – not
with someone else's tongue, will you ever complete
your shattered accident, which is all the splitting
of light might describe – you

find yourself untangling time, looking for where
you left your memorable ending – one of those things
thought you'd lain carefully in a wooden box, only to
find its withered skin propped against the shed

but this is no rotating fan no turn and turn of
the same body – this mind won't catch the same thing
twice, won't replay tunefully, your spine
could be a woodwind, breath raking its golden core

look, you say, the sun – it's about to – and
just in that sequin of molten expectation a tail
surprisingly close to shore rises, then three – *bring
me something to make fire* – we're all looking to ignite our way

splitting light without polite dispersions, without breaking
beams, breaking time, its lighthouse sends out line
after line in the hope of a complete arc – unpick all
the hooks, let all the creatures return to sea

where they can remember the colours of one
another, the gift of broken light – let the shock
of the unborn dead fall into the palms
of their ancestors

let them float the in-between of longing
belonging and never,      let yourself be caught
you've lines over your skin from net, a hook in your lip's
left a navy scar

you practice, squeeze through tiny spaces
crawl along a conviction
you will somehow make it to the edge
back to water

---

Note: With thanks to Marion May Campbell for her translation of
Mallarme's philosophical term, 'scattered accident'.

# metanoia

the book holds the horse – rustling in
there, taking pages between lips, rubbing
upper lip across them, nostrils twin jets
of air as it seeks sweetness

maybe it will kick apart the pages, toss
them into an array, turn a circle and
roll in this dry bedding, maybe it will
stand, wait even when there is no light

for you to open the book, touch immense
warm life within, find its heaving soft coat with
hands, voice – it will come to you, stand patient
while you work out the head-gear, no need for saddle

this is a ride into night sky, bush fragrance leans
into mopoke cries – you stride through leatherwood honey
of wedding bush, long lemon fingers of grevillea, its strange
scent of unwashed male body soaked in maple

scents web themselves over you, languish in your
hair, horse shoulders a deep rhythm in four, walk
with me it says to tiny calling bats, moaning
bronzewings

you're carried to a burial ground – know this
man – he has no grave, murdered his own horse
as it took an apple from his hand, now he takes
breath from the exhalations of the living

being a revenant he pretends at human life, makes
a show of it – gold Mercedes, classical music as he
leans into the bow of road that bends with the river
keeps a bottle of vodka in his work drawer

# margins

at times we find ourselves
at the foot of collapsed futures

we prop, assess panels, draft
another – full of new deletions

we're tired of the big black
circle, the story, collect

all the marks in the margins
of our past, your brave face is

exhausted, sometimes more

all the houses of the past spring
up, our remains

of course, we can't enter – lie
with me, surrender

your upright will for us to make
a cushion under a purring cat

the future doesn't have to be a house
children falling through their own skylights

# the vanished

wood duck on the bend
nape a swan curve looks at a
compression of grey down

# first year

*for G*

you garner courage – up from your
black Broome thongs, oversized shorts
pool-water coloured t-shirt

your body of tears, sways very slightly in the
chair, you seep, your hand on the table under its
weight is tired, waiting

your child, a pavilion of light
has gone into ash, into sea

she lived on the outskirt of herself
perhaps something like the one you
look at us from

you look at us from that outskirt
your eyes the eyes of a child looking
up through water, doesn't know she's

drowning, they're paler, softer
larger than a year ago and you're
without certainty of accomplished
body
language

today language is a river gone
underground – you visit the shore
of her ashes, drink her spiced fuckin
awful rum

she's in your arms in a darkened
room, it's always too late

her molecules rock in the sea, all your
molecules, in salty tears become another
shifting love

we're unreachable to you
wait with you, accompanied by a red
hen who steps around us carefully

she returns, returns, orbiting you
her tight duty to life
making you a wonder to her

# easterlies

across the hills marri flower spectacularly
great creamy clouds of blossom, every tree
vibrating bees, birds busy up there, heads
buried in sticky rings of stamen bristles, sun
dispenses scent of honey

huge pre-dawn easterlies leap
out of the desert, charge, scale the trees
shake and gnaw their clenched fingers, make
them rain dry, dry leaves, drop no-good
into our sleep

body turns away from the howling, forearm
becomes foreleg of a small grey mare
horse body awkward in sheets, long skull
on pillow, hooves scraping linen

and you ...
perched on bed end, smooth feathered belly
wings cup your talons

this adding up to the window broken over
the verandah, so I can run down to join horses
in the hay roll and you can hang over the marri
between your great arms and hunt

# flow

my teacher lifts threads, from a solid
skein, hands them out
after meditation, we offer our forearms
keenly for the red, as though
for a needed transfusion

blessings, tied securely
into a knot on the thread, to be worn
at the pulse of the wrists which frame
steering wheels, stir hot chicken broth into
whisked eggs, console animals in long strokes
sit at the juncture of pulse and action

my father, twenty-four, a military hospital
in Malaysia had several transfusions, his body waxed
then waned against his cancer, blood too white

he gave a life now tied with blood red thread
grace enough to flow

# lead mare

she stands in the quiet of a night
paddock, white coat aglow
breath pulsing cloud, her presence

hugs the house where we sleep, settles
trees disturbed by wind, turtles in the lake

more assured than memory, she presses
her forehead into my chest, I kiss the
velvet cover of each nostril, sweet

humidity of grassy breath, she encompasses
the gifts of the unspoken, her body a wisdom

soft enough to line birds' nests
stride balances earth and sky, mane a script

in my hands, she absorbs my legs, bears me
across, past implied violence of shouting dogs

sound of hooves turning the earth under
them, adjusts the rule of time

# wedding

under a Morton bay fig, roots
as tall as our shins feeling their
way over grass like tentacles of giant
cephalopod

tree an enormous head, veined with fat branches
we stand with empty chip packets, vodka cans
shake cups looped into this creature's arms, arms
implore like an opera singer's – overcome

by the refrain which begins the sequence
of tearing apart

# click

lying in the pit of a night turned
into another gestation, she can't find her
edges in this ink

wind mouths the roof, tries to suck her out
of chrysalis of mattress, pillows, doona, out
into the fresh storm

she coughs, heaves, thinks of the equine
disease, strangles, her air constricts, trachea
twines, tightens and she barks out cough
after cough

there's a tree in her chest, she feels its trunk
resist her sternum, branches reach their tips
into her throat, can't cough it out, is this
the family tree, she wonders

a patient high on pillows, in the pre light for
another icy morning, she wonders if the tree
in her chest can be felled – homeopath

prescribes a high potency – says her line's been
scarred by tuberculosis, radio intones Covid
outbreaks interstate, deaths, thirteen thousand

women buried in roots of her tree sweating, shivering
Hungarian winters, bloody mouths, disease of great
eggs of fluid in their chests, hatch into death carriages
Covid sufferers intubated, comatose, loved ones

in PPE behind glass, goodbyes via videocall, not
knowing if they will surface, hoping, as the doors
of consciousness close behind them, they will
recognize, even in deep state
the click in the lock

# wrong place

this 'underdark' like psychic flywire, pixilating
the view, sips from a wine glass, stands
with its belly pressed into the bar, over the
barmaid in her 'Octoberfest' laced bodice
grinning for a beer

we float on it at night our mattress raft
punted along according to anxious dreams
and scrapping dogs called max

it's a white deposit, a billion white teeth
deep track down into the abyss

seventy-seven-year-old man is killed
by his pet, that roo won't let paramedics
near the dying man, police forced to shoot

tonight a family is waiting for their
child's body to be released, not waiting
for justice

they wait for whatever the sky brings them
– smoking morning, wait for a wind to come
bring a place before the underdark

they shot that roo, the forced police

today's afternoon traffic same as
yesterday's, most who play rat runs across
that dark carry a passenger in the back seat

people will come to do vigil on Monday, stand
in the mouth of this dark with its teeth
of forced police

hope to make some kind
of island

---

Note: *Australian underdark* is a term from D.H Lawrence, *Kangaroo*.

# door of air

eight of us under this ceiling, seven standing, one
supine then four sitting, three standing, one
supine, fingers interlocked over ribcage

seven people whisper among dumplings
of shocked silence, not all of them entered with
us – some were left by the family before, they stumble
over ours as they file out, a rosary of sorrow

room has two lungs, not like a heart
with its lop-sided cross, two lobes, one
curtain, one doorway of air at its left edge

nobody has ever, nor ever will

this division

because a world on one
side dreads the world on the other, though
One is the umbra of the other

this is a case of human
breaking at the threshold
of the door of air

# bardo

hot-bread sky spread with jacaranda silk
petals hang in bunches, cool tender flutes
two weeks ago, these trees were struggling to flower, wettest
November on record, two weeks since the world fell into
water, a season missed its cue

maybe if we get down on hands and knees, crawl
from room to room, carry things in our mouths, on
our backs, we'll be able to connect with how it was
one dropping tears onto tiles while vacuuming, dreams
stretch holes between the living and the dead, one
launders the issues of the other in purple and fawn

you become an ice king, melting inside, weeping
eyes pale as a sky empty of rain, hair turned angelic
silver, you write a letter to your daughter, bronze-wing
snaps its way across the front of the house, camps in
a tree outside the window, hoots its owl moan from
dark to light and back again

we're awash in the bardo, the forty-nine days
prayers, relighting the candle, its mango scent
a kind of shadow

# lady of sorrows

we both see the heart in the eye of the tempest
three swords piercing yes, she says, mater dolorosa
our lady of sorrows

later on the beach, land
birds pose on the sand; wagtail says what are you
going to do about it, wrens pop out of rose geraniums, butterflies
prance in couplet over dune vegetation before their eternal
separation by heavy-breathing wind, imagine all the salt and water
of human tears, anguish roaring up into this wind, gulls spring out
of the way, like marionettes, in distaste

in Zagreb in a tiny alcove off a laneway
women bring their salted lives
into a cavern made hotter with hundreds of fluttering
candles, melted wax shovelled off stone floors like warm
cheese, prayers vie with smoke, stone worn into
knee-shaped hollows

bodies glyph their shameless revelation, this is how
generations creep from hope to
hope, through wars, dictatorship, the ripping of one's
only blanket out of empty hands, the numberless lost

effort of walking here, waiting to enter the flow
of a mercy, to kneel where others might
have received touch, this place like the
womb of the sterile mother, understanding
between women who carry bent bodies onward
into a time where meaning gifts life with life

# golden mala

*for B*

it's been four days since you
left your voice, carried off
in the flood of the stroke
along with upright movement
down the left side

green of your irises does the speaking now, flashes
signals of intensity, sign language of head movements
a nod when asked if you're sleeping ok, no when
asked about pain
your right hand in my left, a golden mala
wound around your forearm

your absent voice hovers in its case of the past, its
clear low tones resonate in auditory recollection
its positive rush, deep tender handling of words, patient
cushioning as it carries a thing of wonder out from
its wet chamber into air

your voice never cut anything
into silence out of spite, it articulated a current of faith, now
that you have resigned it that reassurance is assigned
to the pulsing grip and release of your hand
in mine

so we move into learning how to read all
over again, redirect all focus to facial
each movement a new link in the connection

ignore the strangeness of a room neither
of us have been in before, with its curtain in
front of the door, its unopenable window
the flame tree outside holding a single magpie
stone blue sky, solid with water, bag of amber urine
hanging off this side of your bed

probably the last your partner says
you move nothing in response

# dark of the dark

dark of the moon in the dark
of year, somebody in a Subiaco
subway chanced it, ended up with water
up to their windows, winds tip houses
up-side-down, send them along water
courses, people wake up sailing
in their beds

my two year-old grandson says he's
busting, I take him, sit on a stool in front
of him, hand on his waist, he looks at me
sighs, asks about the pipe leading from
hand basin, I explain – water goes down
the plughole, into the downpipe, up over the bend
through the wall, continues along the side of the house
under the paving, then into underground tank near the
rocks where he was playing
we both sit quietly, then he points to the pipe, says
say again, so we both track a slug of water three more times
I'm finished, he says, leaving nothing

when the other perceives me, it's in reflection
so she'll collect that scrap of something left
in a dream, tiny short sound vocalised in the
root of throat just as body lifts into first
moment of sleep

she was the only one listening as I gave birth, she
was busy dividing the dawn light
in the mirror opposite, impossible
to tell if I was labouring in colour or grey scale –
she ushered in all the visitors, told me
to refuse to make them tea, but I'd lost
too much blood

she walks on the other side of all the aisles
I walk down, has already touched every book I choose, writes
me page after page but they always get waylaid, she
charges the air with patience, counsels my impatience

what did you expect, she asks
braiding the grass with her toes, I say
I wanted to wind up in a lagoon, things settled, everyone
to get out of their nautical beds, find somewhere
to hang their sheets to dry, expect to finally be able
to translate frantic signing of the trees in the wind, for
somebody's, anybody's, wish
to arrive

# renunciation

it was night when her tongue
became a plant, grew out of
itself in fronds, presented buds, made
stems of language into lush shade

it had played long enough with potentials, waited
compliant in its cave of vows, but the waters
it sat in were thick with the anaerobic chemistry
of these things, it wanted to cry out, find a company
of ears, dance with those winds of voice
trained for silence

it talked in her sleep, told the quiet
room this was not the place for her, not the right kind
of ears here, when something alighted, sipped nectar
it became a plant, unconcerned with crooked
channels of silence, finding its veins flowing from a
different source, girdle torn open, binding fallen
away, window something to pour through

as plant it chooses to be more tender, relinquish
questions of voice and expression, to wait, partake
of coolness, of sweetness and oh the green

this is how she gave up trying to breathe under pressure, see
behind walls, walk blindfolded, by a kind of lucid
sensuality, by reaching anyway

# because you died

vanishing into
hospital linen,   antiseptic        emptiness
air became realised against
skin, everybody's faces became somebody
else

as soon as there was running there was
running to her, as soon as there was
waiting it was behind a door she'd
just closed, as soon as the light switch
snapped all to blackness her drift up
the hallway showered in light had to
be imagined

all things estranged themselves, television
seemed to animate an unreadable
context, roses in the carpet stopped
growing, cream telephone in the hall
screaming then forgetting what it wanted

outside on grass desiccated by sun, chickens
tried to use wings but couldn't stop
making excuses, swing in the yard tipped
the sky off its shelf on each attempt to
stay on the plank
find the latch on the gate follow her
trees fragrant with peppercorn and resin
push sky back up on its shelf, walk
into a Christmas spider, it sticks to singlet

centre of chest

a Carnaby turns and turns on its branch, see
the way for it to reach little cones it's bobbing for
watch with spider, wait for the bird to pivot over
branch, white tail see-saws upward, two spoons
of its beak pincers the cone

because you died there's an oblong
hole, in sand, to the right of every
interior

she is upstairs asleep under fawn blanket
curled on her right side – her want to be
here gone, out the door, running
on the beach, looking for the ribbon
that joins sky to sea

# her god way

when I stepped out of fear, her god way
with me settled, come to think of her
as a water creature, something huge stroking
from north pole to south in little more than a
season, largest brain on the planet, crying
crying out into water all she knows

it's said she endures torturous
headaches, she's been known to smoke, but
sees with an eye the size of my
house and her concern with the human, is
an agony without relief

yet she's sure of
herself, suspended at the end of
light, each crimson limb stirs
its own slow current, can configure a whole
architecture of community and politic
instantaneously; intimately

wise scope of her makes sea lice of us, requires
respectful distance to avoid paralysis
she incorporates the wild so has no need of humility

its bright beams make a dandelion of me at the
imagining of any interaction, diminished
and celebrated simultaneously, but she
wants me to share what it's like to walk
in ancient dust, to work out how to make
alms from a small life, to encourage
someone to give up doing it alone

# stage four

*for A*

each word comes slowed, dispensed
as cleanly as a coin in its return chute

they've made a mask of your face, to
hold you motionless for radiation

therapy, targeted two points of your brain
oncologist talks of spot welding

two women work a perfect choreography
to net your face, map its coordinates

in a week red gerbera on your table's collapsed
your handwriting's become someone else's

you're both who you've always been and
the systemic chaos of your illness

you arbitrate upon the fulcrum between
past and future, listing to the right, between

not caring enough and resolutely
mothering this array of choices

you pave your own track out
we wind up its spiral stair

thoughts of chairlift and a fire pole
pull logic in different directions

# boulders

For two nights I've dreamt about pale blue waters that should have been clear, the kind of waters found in mountain country; waters from snow melt, lightly infused with copper so the blue is jewel-melt, streaming. These dream waters were distorted by boulders, that's how it is; flow will make its way through, even if it takes generations.

June 24, 1977, mum and I in a friend's holiday house in Guilderton, a tiny estuary hamlet up the coast. Isabelle was with us, the mint green miniature Queenslander belonged to her parents. She had knees as wide as her thighs, walked with a ballet dancer gait and her first love was her lemon tree, who she talked to every day and from whom she once received a one pound lemon. She and I slept on a pine bunk bed in a room the size of a cubicle. Early winter light, condensation on the window, an extended family of New Holland honey eaters in the weeping peppermint tree outside, and a solitary magpie. Air inside humidifying with bacon and buttered toast vapours. Mum woke us with a call to breakfast and we were stacking the plates with smears of egg, tomato juice and toast corners when I remembered her birthday, thirty-six. Shame dimmed the room. Breakfast in bed for her was my priority on special days, though mum often worked two or three jobs and was a drinker, so the morning tray never drew anything like this hungry appreciation. She shook her head at my sorry words, enjoying the trick of it.

Isabelle and I walked the long, fat sand track to the beach. The sea, alive and reaching high onto the caramel shore, was changing from blue to green. We headed to the groyne, both our bodies stopped walking in the same second. There were five older boys on the giant rocks, probably seventeen, eighteen years to our thirteen. We turned left in duet, marched straight in a trajectory, right angle to the groyne, and up the beach. We fell into the arms of the waves, swam just beyond our depth, backflips, handstands, Isabelle teaching butterfly. I tried again and again to float, bum always sank, sun flaring my vision, feet settled on sand, Isabelle swimming straight at me, crying, those boys are on our towels. I saw the fringe of cold beach, empty but for our scrappy towels and strangers lounging on them.

Fuck, what do we do! I looked out to sea, up into the sky, down into the green underwater sand. And the sky, sea and sand said, hide . . . behind the waves. So that's what we did, diving under just as the wave in front flattened, coming up for breath when the next ridge formed between us and the beach. Breath by breath we moved towards the river mouth, until we were far enough away to swim in unseen, run up the dunes.

By then the boys were starting to look for us, two of them standing, shading their eyes in salute, searching the water. We ran back to the house, without clothes, shivering pale chicken skin, trying for air as desperately as landed fish, translucent feet jabbed by the sharp stony gravel. Isabelle's parents had arrived. Her father called us stupid, shouted, drove us back to get our towels. We sat in the back sniffing salt water, hair dripping. The boys were still there. They said nothing. He said nothing. Boulders.

# light is no longer visiting

When it left it made the air into a soft sorrow and just as this hard cold began its sinking the wrens threw out a fretful spray of squeaking questions. The pink and grey galahs unhinged their cries as they swung over the paddocks to roost in the lemon-scented gum at the bottom of the driveway. That great candelabrum of limbs has more rooms than our house. The sky over the roof has five stars pressed into it.

Outside the guardians are shushing the air, their bodies living out a patience entirely attendant upon the sun. I put thick socks on and then buckle my feet into solid coverings so that I can cope with the stones and gravel. I make my way between these living stretches, palms cupping them for balance.

Last January we visited a hundred-year-old redwood forest, walked storeys high on metal bridges and ramps suspended through standing trunks. There were signs asking not to touch the bark. It was thick and fibrous like softer jarrah bark. The hands wanted to find where the softness receded, as they might seek to measure the depth of a bear pelt.

Over three hundred people queued on the ground in a decomposing snake of human parts, waiting their turn to mount the ramps, float with the lanterns through the standing ones, consider the sentient might of a two thousand year-old relative in California by comparison. We didn't touch – we wanted these chestnut-skinned siblings of time to reach magnificence.

These ones I can touch, am known to them; have chewed the sap of the massive marri that waits by the house, rescued the cat out of the arms of its partner by standing on the stable roof holding a plank under a branch. These and a hundred others have stood through many light cycles, sometimes staying quiet while we sleep, sometimes whooshing the roar of desert winds to the coast in a wrestle that strips their leaves more greedily than an autumn storm.

# light slices the room

Light slices the room like a series of chimes, moon pressure fingers the
windows, burrows deeper into pillows like a hump-backed marsupial,
snuffles out snatches of dream remnants – a girl has become critical, a
man I once knew who hated innocence, walks around a perfect square
of very cold, very dark water. I wait for you to begin the day by taking
the dogs out into dark frogcall. They have something to say to this
moon, want to inspect the shimmer she's left in everything wet, see
which of her twenty-eight houses she has caravanned past in the night.
Itinerant Baba Yaga, resistant to letting hope settle, she's climbed all
over the roof, testing how deeply asleep we might be, pretended to be
you getting up for the dogs – so we surprised each other in the laundry.

Was a time I wondered if I belonged to her, not that those were mother
issues but she assures me I do not . . . but my mother did. She was a
little moon child with a smile wider than a window. She used it as
a charm to climb into people's lives when she wanted to leave her
own. Once she was roaming the square of her home village, Pozega,
wandering to keep herself from the chill of the only child. She heard
the churning of a wedding going on at the church, went up the steps,
and watched the ceremony from the portico. When the couple returned
up the aisle to enter the evening she took the bride's hand and told
her she was the most beautiful woman she had ever seen. When the
bride thanked her, she asked if she could go to the wedding feast – so
hours later her mother, searching door to door, found her dancing at a
wedding.

# tonight we'll set a place

Tonight we'll set a place for you. It's pumpkin soup and toast, but there'll be a slice of cinnamon banana teacake, made with allspice instead, as the cinnamon could not be found. A glass of golden liquor, scotch or Drambuie, gold for the smile between the sun and the moon, so tenderly sought between the blades of this midwinter dark. A candle will be lit and we'll float our love on phrases connected to what we knew of you. A will talk about you giving her ice cream, and for me the boarded-up chest of unease – a memory of you with tears glazing your eyes as you describe how sweetly your three-year-old granddaughter asks for ice cream, how she takes your face in her hands, kisses one cheek and when you open your full moon smile, she asks, says please. It was a period when we were keeping sugar out of her diet – and one of those times we sat together without answers.

It seems you had something of an underground life, not only being different with different people, but being a miner, taking found tools and making instruments of direction with them, magnetising them according to need. On becoming a widow at twenty-four you made yourself into someone who could manage the stricken load of two dependents, dropped like meteors out of context, not that you wanted to. Then at your next engagement party a six-foot tall woman tripped, holding a plate of sausages out to your three-year old and crushed me against a wine glass. You took me to hospital to have my head stitched.

You dug up the leach drain in our back yard, moved the pond by yourself, did your own tree-lopping and still you tracked something deep – kept a journal when you went back to Croatia in your late fifties, the writing didn't seem to come the way you wanted it to but the living did. Every so often you would find something, a precious luminous creature of your underground light.

# yesterday and tomorrow

Yesterday I am having dinner with an old friend, a sometime mentor, in a February Melbourne apartment. The night, relieved of light, is deep, soup-warm, a floating moon two per cent off full. We are up in my absent sister-in-law's apartment, I tell P about a dream I had about him teaching me the rules of poetry, which in the dream is exactly like teaching me how to play cricket, he is telling me his life in edits, adding the details affection demands. We both look through the big rectangle of glass displaying the night, as though the portraits of those he loves were visible there.

Tomorrow the same friend guides me through the central grid of Melbourne. I have been up most of the night with my sister-in-law's boyfriend, arrived from Hungary just last night, thirty-six hours to cross the world. His first ever green curry has him pausing to savour, we make a fairground of the Victoria Markets, buy gifts for home; tie-dyed overalls for my teenager, yappy mechanical puppy for our four-year-old, a white cotton button-less shirt. We meet for the first time around 3.00 pm and sometime after 10.00 pm I knock on his door to apologise, ask for help because my life has just detonated via a phone call. He hugs me, says let's go for a walk. We walk for five hours through streets neither of us know. This city's face glows sweetly for him, just inside the portico of a new relationship, his chest fairly bursting with it, overlooks me, staggering through interior rubble, hollowed out by shock.

A possum the size of a spaniel sits up on one of the paths veining Carlton Gardens, solemnly watches us trace patterns over the ground under an overblown moon, make other patterns, criss-crossed with the pictures of the past each of us is made of, we try for sleep after three.

In grey light I run a bath, pouring what oils I find; olive, lavender. Water, a resting place, cushions slack aching weight, mind banging against skull, trying for ways out, then falling as far as Icarus into a bathtub, back to staring at the heater light, windowless room a chamber, sounds of water pouring away from shifting limbs. Will forces the mind to order; there was a café meeting at 9.30. Catch a tram down Spencer Street, buy rescue remedy. Incoherent as any accident victim, it takes as much focus to purchase a tram ticket as it does to cook a meal. Hear need in my own voice when I request the remedy, a choice between drops and pastilles, pay for both, walk back up Spencer Street, past a powder-blue bicycle frame, memorial to cyclists killed inside the city grid, past a street artist, something happening to sight, can't remove sunglasses, avoid observing reflection in the acre of plate glass, at traffic light rely on sound, the whoosh of fellow pedestrians, make it to P at the café.

After coffee, no food, no food, he ushers me on a straight unhurried walk to St Paul's. He could be a tenor, his voice, tempered as resin, smooth as deeply polished wood, burbles us along, his upper arm presses into mine, releases, the living warmth of his voice now connects me to what had once been a life of my own. I listen passively and move my feet, aware that pieces of me are breaking off, floating out of reach, inner vision too fades to empty, the future ceases on hallowed ground.

# god

The pool I swam in last night was rectangular, one of those very rare
pools dark with fresh clear water. Two living things: a small octopus
and a fish. The fish had two broad sides, its lips taking up the width of
its face, each eye looking away from its head at a completely different
perspective. Octopus is vastly accomplished in comparison, graceful,
complete. Any more than two arms and you're a god. Wisdom's own eye
roaming a face without symmetry – but more by way of exemption than
misfortune, as if she had the freedom to decree 'No, my eyes will not be
stuck with this view of underwater light with a single fish swimming in
it, my eyes will roam my head because it must flow with three hearts
and ten nervous systems. Eighth arm a special stethoscope, its tip
reaching to detect the state of a heart. We swam in that pool, three of us
~~peacefully~~ moving as if we were breathing absinthe, water on skin cool
as white linen, the scene completely without any push for purpose, as
though the aggregates of any creature and the world could simply add
up to kindness.

# what did you do with your Sappho?

Are her texts unruptured, performed in schools, is hers among the popular baby names, is she quoted by writers and at meetings, have her words lubricated your languages, have they gone deep into the continents, is her music performed by choirs at festivals, do the paintings in the halls dramatise her life, does every dawn wear sandals, do the muses leave gifts at her steps, is there a reading of person or character under her name, is she alive in the sapphic adjective, sapphic verse, do you have sap-dance

Has she brought out in your humanity the ability to hold eye contact in the presence of a beloved, and does she stand as the third presence between every pair of beloved friends, how do you remember her and what seats are reserved for her, is there a honey named after her, a flower that blooms at night and holds open its petals for the arrival of light, and of course your daughters are skilled with the weaving techniques of eros, no coarse imitation, no insincere cries, but the laughing talk of the free, courage of her lioness heart
Her words weave the emptiness, even as they've been flayed by some worlds to a clutch of fragments, withstood the derision of historians and gossiping citizens

What is *whiter by far than an egg,* do women write, do they strain to hear her through the bars of broken poems, secretly converse with her memory?

Is it illegal for them to congregate, have they accepted solitudes, are they given the roles of the menial, is it auspicious to see a woman standing with her daughters, is the birth of a daughter celebrated, is one sister left, alone, in your Pleiadean stories

# SAPPHO'S GIFT
## A POETICS OF THE FRAGMENT

Language authors me and others in relation to me. The pen is a lit
match. Within a finite time period that flame is going to injure. So,
here's the imperative to keep moving – because words have a short half-
life, they function within a dynamic context.

Fragmented writing enacts its own breaking/loss and so the effects of
trauma, shock, violences of speaking and silence are evidenced on the
page. Each fragment augments and is augmented by the historical,
syntactic and physical space between itself and other fragments.

Through mimetic performance the subject who writes, reads, witnesses
herself in fragmentation. There is trauma, loss, the abyss, and there
is something else also, a coexistence of the fragments in a shared
proximity. This – proximity is crucial, even where it is the result of
random cause it culminates in the particular.

The fragment accentuates the break each story makes with its own
narrative stability. In truth any story is told in the faery tale register –
an unpacked preface could read; If such a thing as an unbroken story
could be told, this is how it might happen; once upon a time . . .
And we know how the forces of myth are woven through faery tale
via the detail that sits uneasy, often through syntax, as an unbroken
surface – the stepsisters who cut parts off their feet to fit the shoe.
Uneasy because we cut parts of ourselves, the other, to fit the story.

The writing acknowledges the split subject, the subject maintained and
lost amongst an infinite variation of fragmented narrative. The stories
may be trans-generational, but are located in a common temporal space

because of trauma, contradiction and loss. The way these ruptures disrupt temporal linear narrative corresponds to timeless space.

The address to the reader, to borrow a term from film studies, is a direct address. It breaks the silence between the text and the reader, marks the text as reader-aware, and suggests the writing as a space of co-creation.

What is the loss of the 'other' where I am lost to myself, where memory and writing are weak links that rely on the grief of my body, my body crying out like an Orphic head – those tales where a body part will not cease uttering the fragments and their stories – the possibility of an original time that could perhaps heal the raw edges of never being the same again.

I write amongst the fragments, test their edges on the soft rim of my heart.

Fragments taunt with half-promises of narratorial commitment. We are almost-free in the almost-possible. The memory of this moment will fracture in time when the cost of its exclusive coherence comes to bear. A spider just walked across this page, having rushed out of The Sin of the Book.

Virginia Woolf won't look at me. In her throat there is sealed a box with a pained embryonic thing – a woman with her arms by her side, head dropped forward onto her chest, her breasts out of alignment and falling as she tries through sheer will to bring herself into focus.

Consider undressing – not for the sake of any eyes. Pupils are holes, they emit no-one. Between their fluctuations (it is said) is the locus of the soul; naked, waiting long since before your hands found this page.

There are events to which I am connected, as the child of an immigrant, but which I am alienated from. They augment and parallel the psychic, psychological and historical life of everything written and spoken.

The fragment is compassionate with her. Here she can write, here she can be meaningless and be considered invaluable. The fragment accepts her wounding, shows her how to bear it, reference its mystery.

Mystery because the fragment can't be resolved. Its shores dissolve into the sublime, the unspeakable and she is not the same again because of this fragment.

There is no measure here that will reduce this space. There is no measure that will enlarge it. It is consistently itself and aspires to nothing but to know itself and become.

She writes herself into a life which has already torn who she is. The tearing precedes her. She is born into the scene where her being is impossible. She writes onto the backdrop of everything she might become.

There is randomness. Telos – multiple, infinite. The point to begin with is this point, this moment. Take this moment, its composition of fragmented memory, narrative, sentences and conversations, dream pieces and write from that. Don't question, don't edit, just write what is.

The writing itself is the site of surrender, of risking not only garment but skin and organs, stripping down to the unstable, partial, multiple psychic trembling. One cannot pass through intact. Yet it links into the timeless space of all possibility.

Because she can cross into these fragments, she is also other to them.

Her life is composed of the psychic substance of many lives, shaped by traumas and choices made generations before she was born, and it is also other to them. Her life is hers to create, to write, to live simultaneously.

Her otherness, it ushers itself through the shared compassion of the fragmented space. In the fragment nobody escapes the loss. It's a narrative of loss, it performs the rent. It is also the source of absolute compassion. It is the moment when having lost all, each takes a spoon and dips it into the pot of beans, boiled in salt water, in silence. It has no past and no future.

This space is alert, sensitive, both to itself and to all other than itself. It is ready to extend in any direction, to undo all that has begun within it. It remains poised in a moment that is immediate and timeless – because of its responsiveness to all.

It aspires to nothing but to know itself and become, and here there is a sense of poetry. Made of language, the fragment reaches from the unlocatable centre of each word toward a more poetic realisation, without judgement and in welcome to the other.

She exceeds the writing and is unattainable to herself outside the writing. It is the physical and psychic enactment of her selfhood. It is the place of being and of witnessing; a reformation, a voice calling into the storm of torn fragments of her subjectivity. Perpetually she is recomposed, not a dismemberment realigned, not made into any whole, but alive in relation to each fragment, for her voice has moved through them all.

This is a shared space. It allows sharing with respect to the other. Each fragment is augmented by this relationship making no claim on the other or the unspeakable, it simply allows space on the page, between words, within the word, for difference.

A word like broken suggests something with a clean edge, where the edge marks a separation, an absolute distinction between a form and its absence. Language has edges made of resonances. They are both physical, (auditory), and philosophical (impacting meaning). One of my students begins her piece of writing with the click of a cassette recorder at the end of a tape. In doing so she begins with the effect of resonance. The harsh mechanical break charges silence with the resonance of what might have gone before. A fragment can be torn, shaved, skimmed, cut, crumbled – it can be anything where language refers to its own partiality. There are no dominant metaphors. It may not always have a clean edge, but it always trips multiple resonances.

Our questioning comes from a traumatised place, seeks an accountable other. She pursues that which is unbearable to her, herself disappearing and appearing among fragments.

In choosing to write, she chooses to witness the narratives and fragments of her subjectivity. She witnesses the rites her great grandmother performs against the illnesses of her dying children, her mother as a child – hiding in the chook pen to watch the chickens lay their eggs. These scenes are part of her substance, her 'tissue'. They may be 'pictograms' enlarged by her imagining; they may be the charge of an unconscious that works 'like a language'. They become the body of her identity.

In the writing, though she must cross the abyss, the white space, the void where she risks meaninglessness, she acquires substance in the operations of the fragment. The writing of herself is both imaginary and literal. She simultaneously writes the novel, entering into fiction.

She is the main character writing herself, negotiating the space of the fragment with the reader.

She cannot access the assured 'I', even as a fallible construct. She finds herself choosing to face the full extent of existential loss, the fragmentation of the contemporary subject, because therein is the chance that meaning, however precarious might return to her. She says, *i know i can only haunt this space, i am displaced many times over, but the attempt will transform the field for myself and the other and the others of myself and even that is enough.*

The faith in this gesture affirms life, is akin to the intake of a breath. We do it, for the moment, whatever this moment makes of us and whether this moment takes place consciously or unconsciously.

The fragment is nothing if not beautiful. It is true philosophy. It seeks to know itself, to loving each word to a consciousness of its history – history being all the contexts of its articulation. It has the strength of all time, language through time, tempered by all the lives it has entered. Only lived language can be this beautiful.

This is a vigilant space, where the silences, the spaces where word is absent, hold their charge and direct it to the heart of the accountable moment. We look for meaning in the space between the signifier and the signified. It is the one place where it might happen and the waiting for meaning's signal, or its other, demands courage.

We wait as we would for a possible meeting with a lover. There will be a fall, sooner or later, but for now even the stars might be signaling me.

If the fragment is a site where ancestral, psychic layers bleed through, a site of mourning, of such longing that even now as I draw my pen over paper my centre is tight with the pangs. This is the longing that makes us hide in language – we hold words over ourselves like orangutans hold giant leaves, or if they're zoo animals, canvas sheets, in a downpour. We hide our eyes, our senses.

The cry at birth must have been the word for this loss.

I look for it, long for it, dig for it through my very body with my pen, my hand shaping word after word. Something is touched by this loving gesture where the other will seek me and reach for me and that reaching will make a space that might enable me to say I am this, this moment with you – our longing has created this present in language to be for a time.

What happens to the writer as she writes? What does the fragment demand of her? There may be some experiences which are partially mine, partially because they can never enter language fully, and they are reconstructed by the demands of the text.

The writer is a peacemaker. She isn't a 'real' writer, a disembodied persona that accompanies a best seller like a complimentary bookmark. She is the writer who 'writes to survive'.

She can make peace with the words because she is only just born of them at any point in the     .